Inside Eye™

AMAZING ANIMALS

This edition first published in MMXV by
Book House

Distributed by Black Rabbit Books
P.O. Box 3263
Mankato
Minnesota MN 56002

Printed in the United States of America.
Printed on paper from sustainable forests.

Cataloging-in-Publication Data is available from the Library of Congress

ISBN: 978-1-906370-73-2

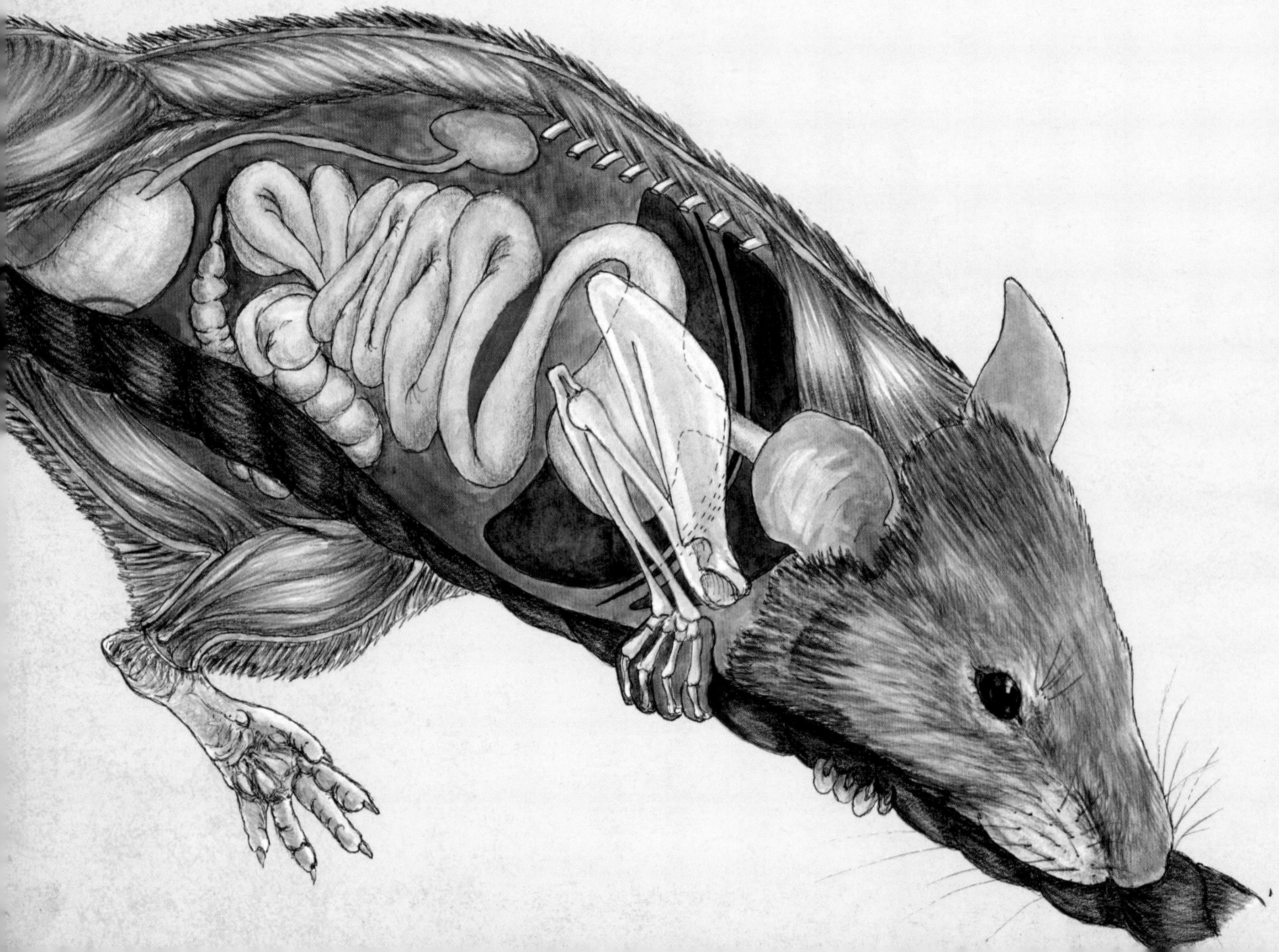

Inside Eye™

AMAZING ANIMALS

Written by
Margot Channing

CONTENTS

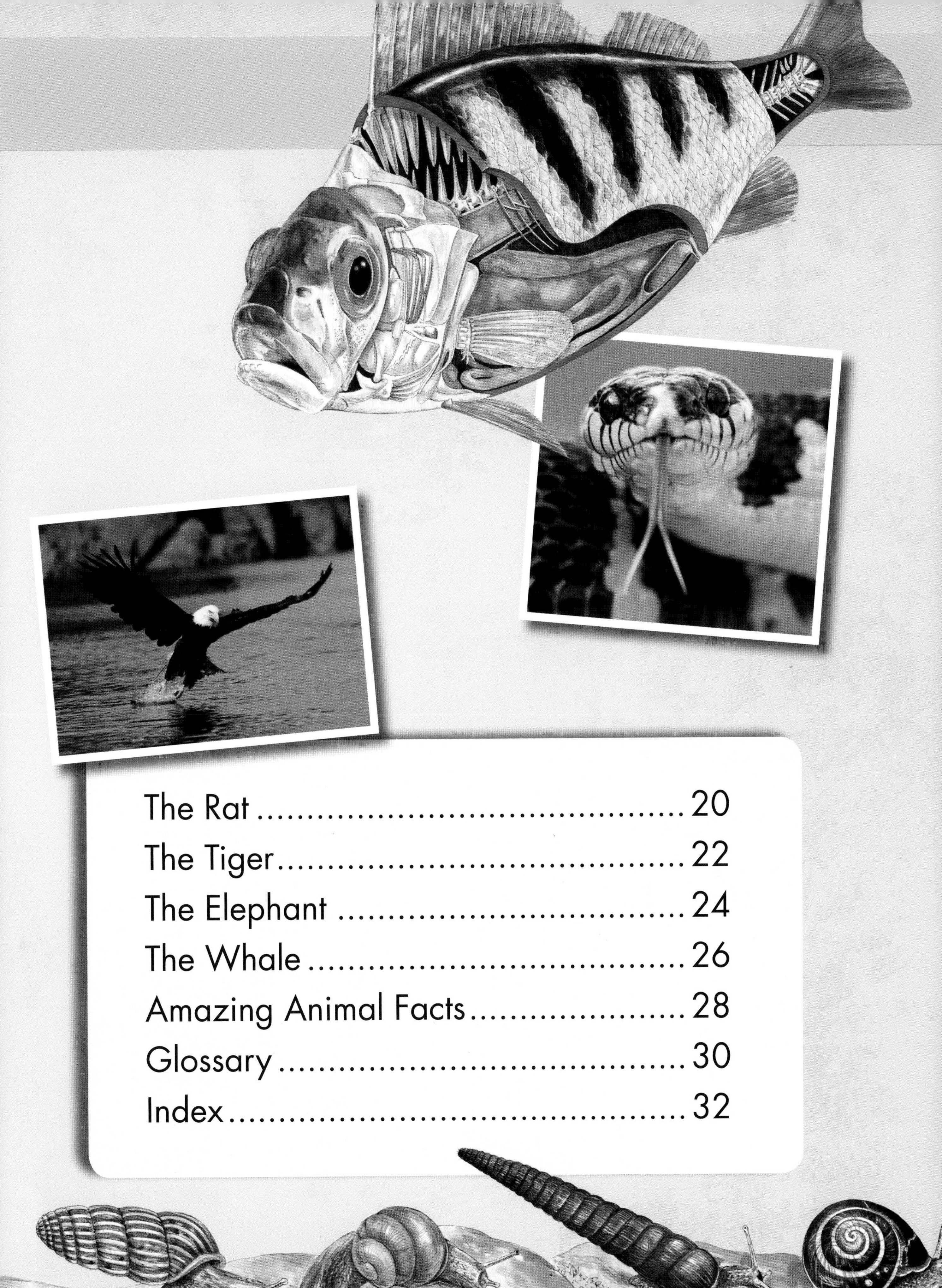

The Animal World

Animals are amazing. There are many different species, or types, of animals on Earth. The ocean is full of whales, dolphins, fish, and seals. On land there is a wide range of monkeys and apes, big cats, bears, snakes, and many more animals. Birds soar high in the sky above Earth and fish swim in our rivers, lakes, and oceans.

The lion is a big cat. It is one of Earth's most powerful predators.

The hippopotamus is a river-living creature. It has extremely powerful jaws.

Naming Animals

There are so many different types of animals in our world that scientists have created a system to help us identify them. It is called classification. We group different types of animals according to their appearance and body structure. There are seven main animal groups. They are: insects, mollusks, amphibians, fish, reptiles, birds, and mammals.

Inside Eye

In this book, we will look at animals from each group to discover what they look like, where they live, what they eat, and much more. And with an amazing "inside eye" and stunning cutaway illustrations, we'll show you exactly what each animal looks like—from the inside out.

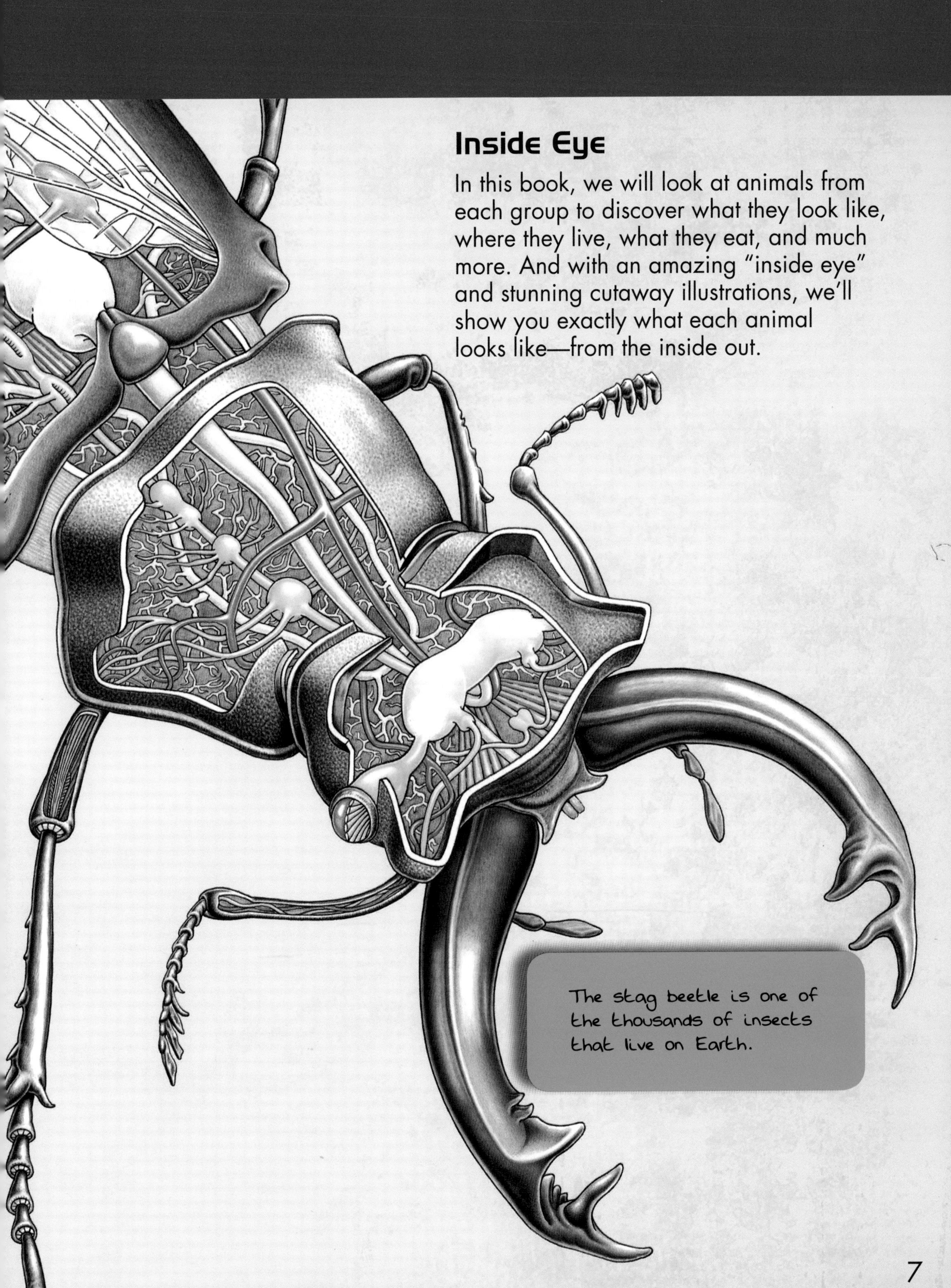

The stag beetle is one of the thousands of insects that live on Earth.

The Fly

The fly is an insect with two wings. It also has a pair of winglike structures called halters. These help it balance so that it can fly straight and level. Flies are super aeronauts—they can fly forward, sideways, and upside down. They can even land upside down on a ceiling!

Dirty Flies

The housefly has been shown to spread several human diseases. Flies like to feed on rotting food in trash cans and also on fresh food left uncovered in the kitchen. Flies particularly like sweet, sticky foods.

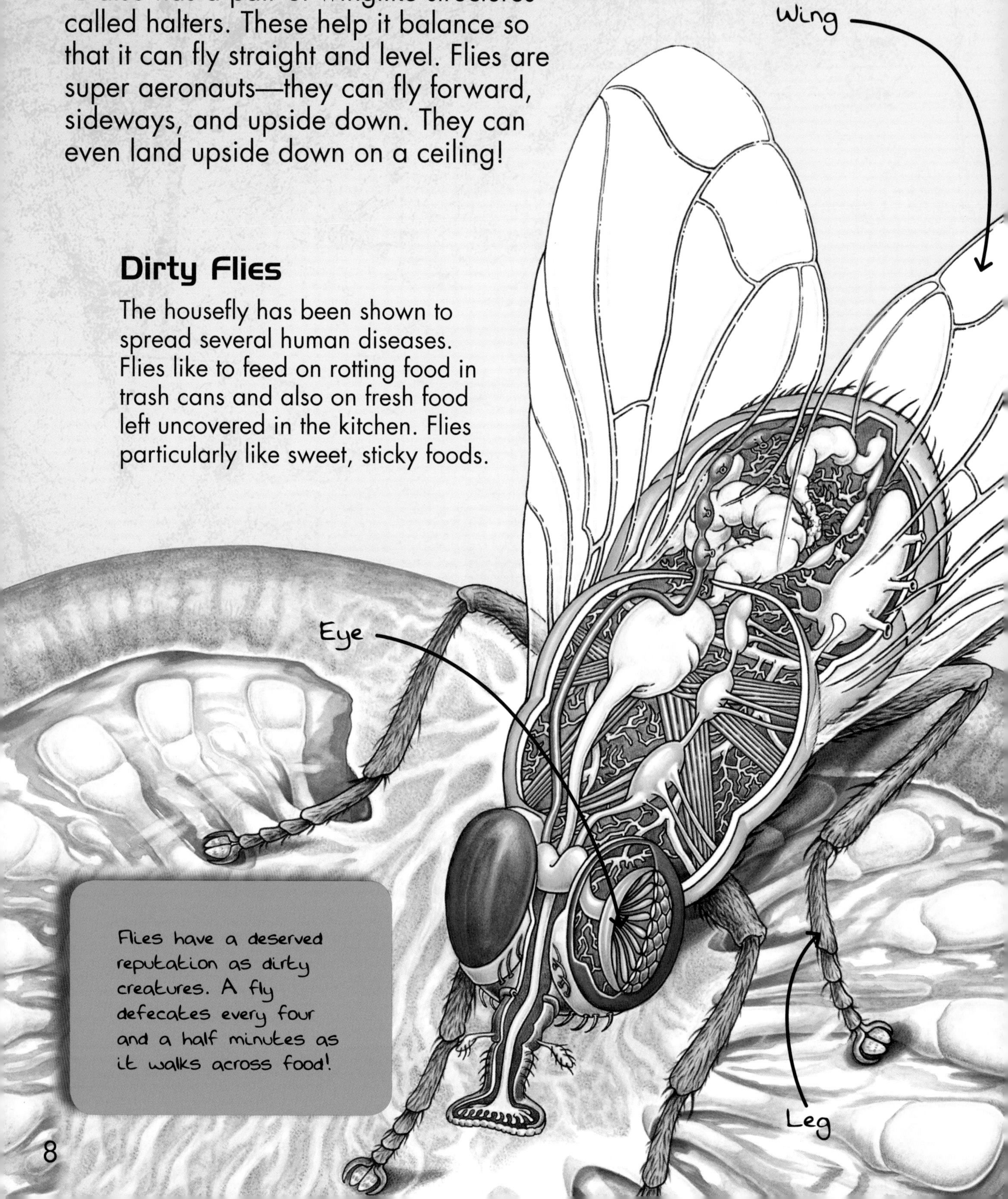

Flies have a deserved reputation as dirty creatures. A fly defecates every four and a half minutes as it walks across food!

Although it seems disgusting that flies lay their eggs in dead bodies, this practice does perform a vital role in clearing up dead matter.

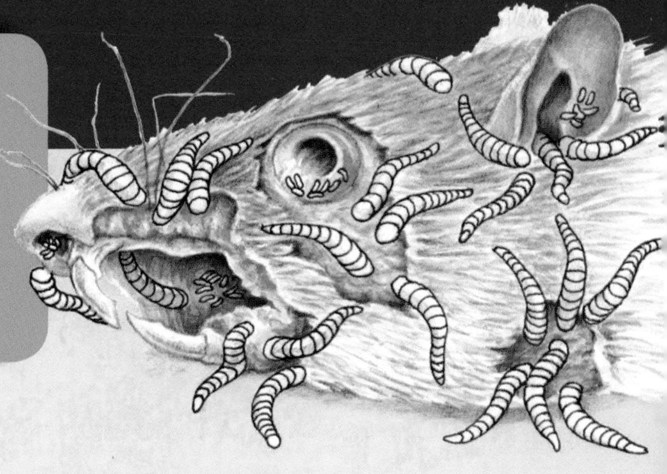

Nature's Cleaners

Flies are very important to nature. They lay batches of up to 150 eggs on dead animals. The eggs hatch into maggots, which then eat away the remains of the animal. This removes waste quickly and efficiently.

The fly's ability to move swiftly and easily is due to its multijointed legs and its foot pads, which even enable it to walk upside down on ceilings.
The hairs on the fly's legs act as sense organs and it also has taste buds in its feet.

Foot

Fly Eye

The fly's bulging eye is made up of thousands of tiny lenses. These lenses give it superb all-round vision and are especially sensitive to movement. The fly can see a flyswatter coming and escapes!

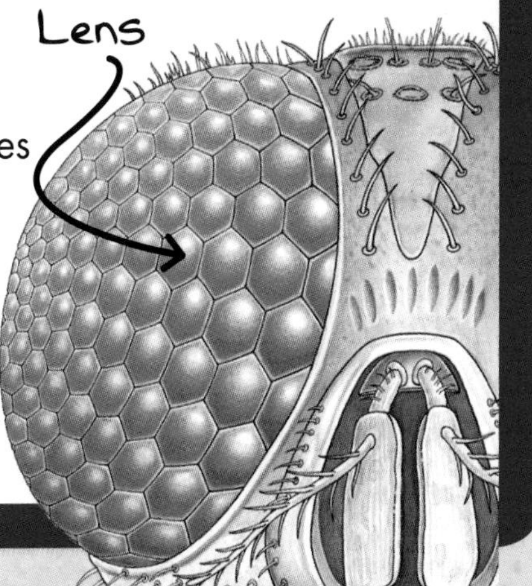

The Snail

The snail is a mollusk. It has a soft body that is covered by a sheet of tissue called the "mantle." It has a shell—a hard covering that protects and houses the soft body beneath. The snail is a gastropod, which means "foot-stomach." It is so named because it appears to walk on its stomach.

A mollusk's shell has a horny outer layer that is reinforced with inner layers of calcium carbonate. Secretions of calcium carbonate from beneath the shell increase its thickness.

At Home Anywhere

Carrying their homes on their backs, snails are found almost anywhere. The snail's body, including its intestine, follows the contours of its spiralling shell. The shell can spiral to the left or to the right.

Muscle Foot

The snail has a very muscular underside, or foot. The muscles ripple back and forth to move the snail forward across a surface.

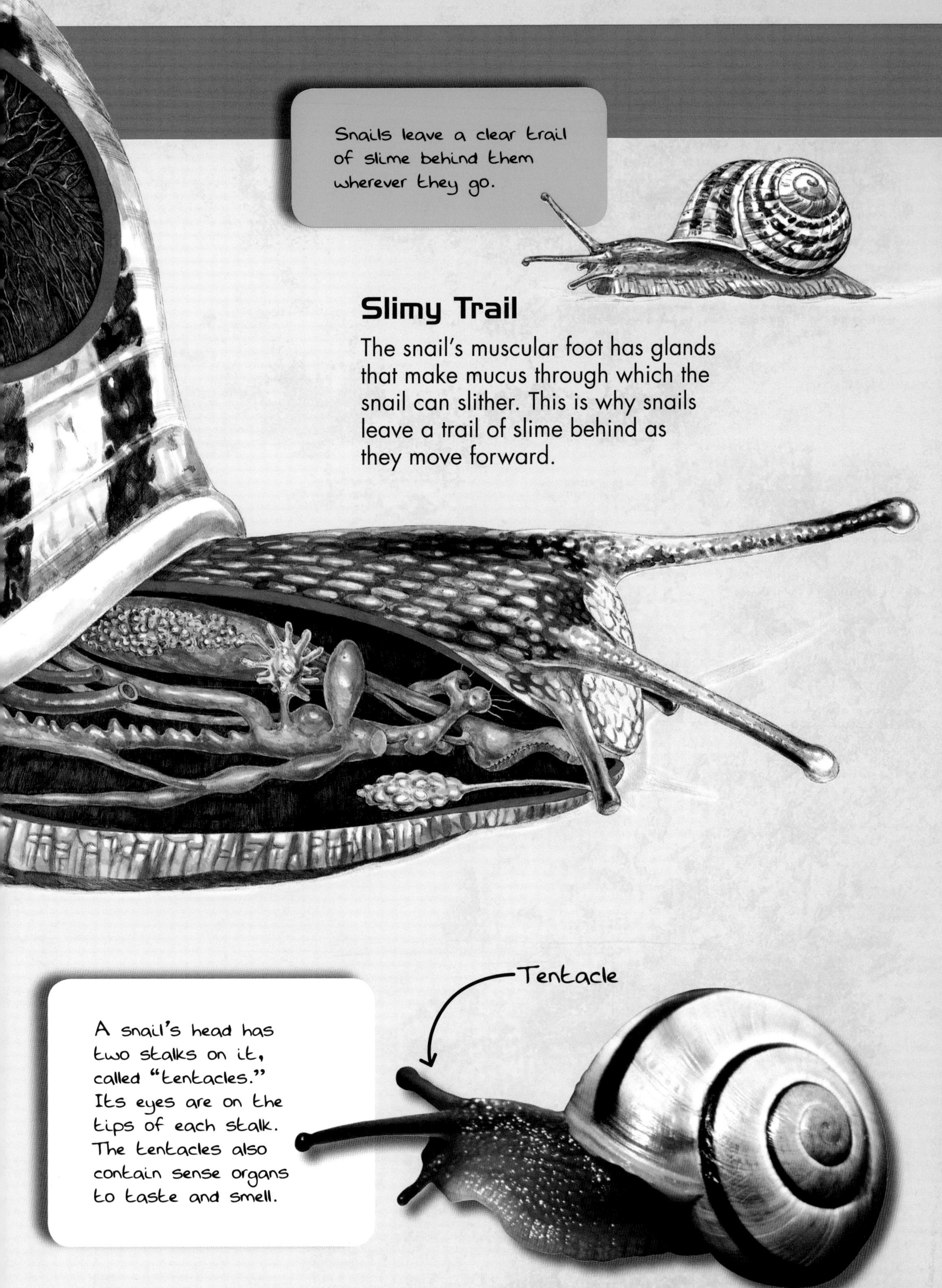

Snails leave a clear trail of slime behind them wherever they go.
Tentacle
A snail's head has two stalks on it, called "tentacles." Its eyes are on the tips of each stalk. The tentacles also contain sense organs to taste and smell.

Slimy Trail

The snail's muscular foot has glands that make mucus through which the snail can slither. This is why snails leave a trail of slime behind as they move forward.

The Frog

The frog is probably the most successful of all amphibians. Frogs are found all over the world. They live in damp places such as marshes and ponds. Frogs catch insects, worms, and slugs using their sticky tongue, which is attached to the front of the mouth. The frog flicks out its tongue, catches its prey, and then returns it to its mouth to swallow it.

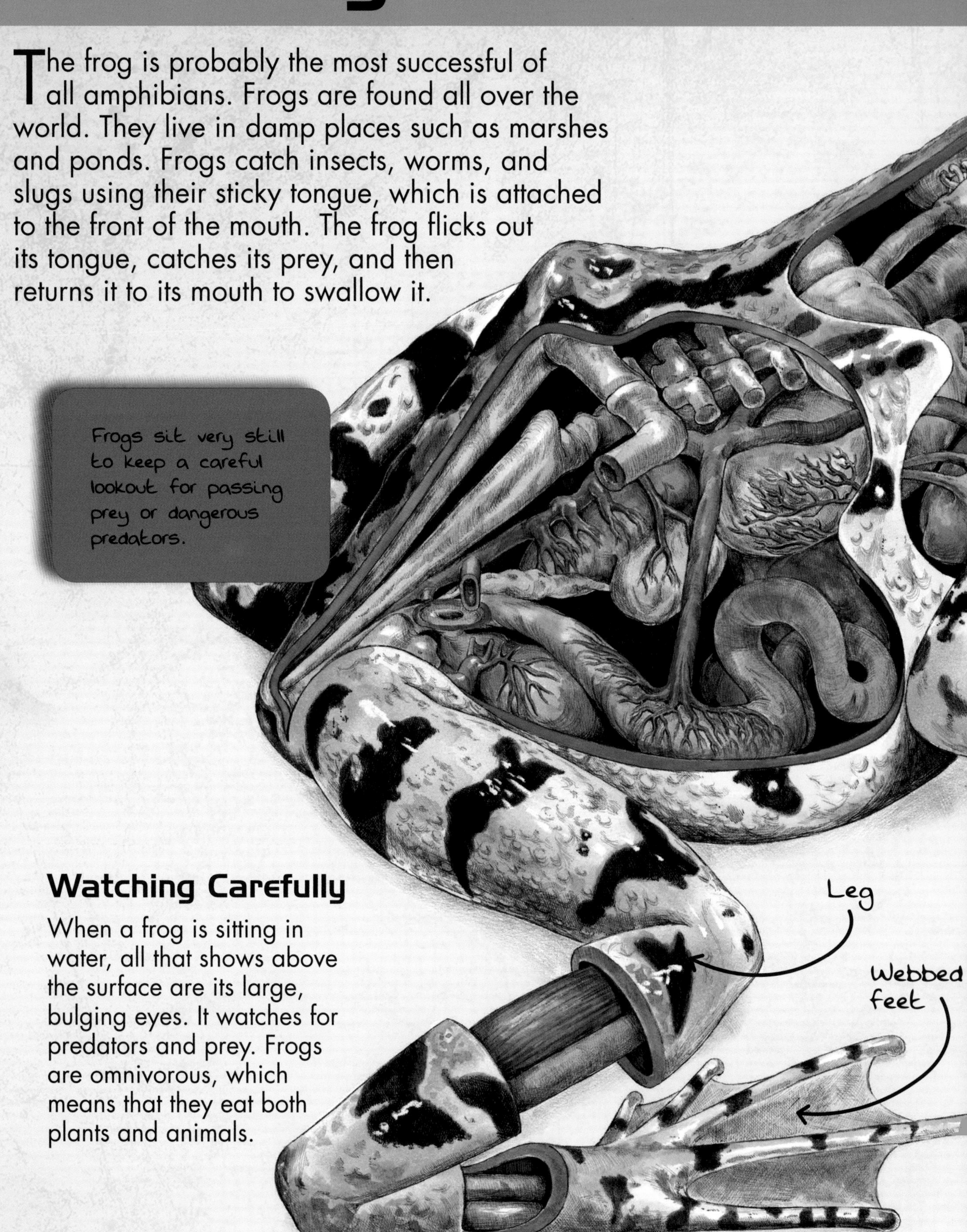

Frogs sit very still to keep a careful lookout for passing prey or dangerous predators.

Watching Carefully

When a frog is sitting in water, all that shows above the surface are its large, bulging eyes. It watches for predators and prey. Frogs are omnivorous, which means that they eat both plants and animals.

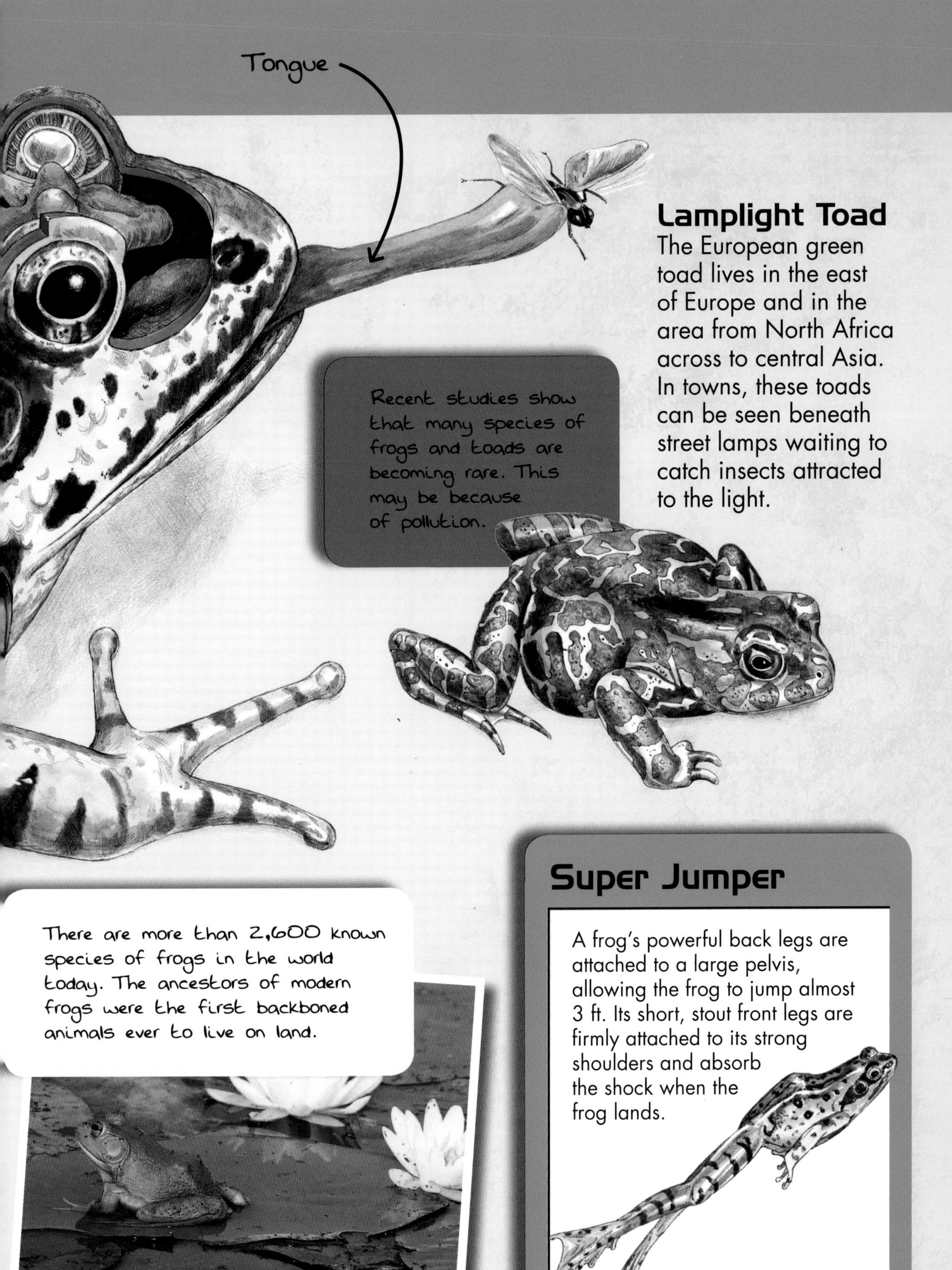

Recent studies show that many species of frogs and toads are becoming rare. This may be because of pollution.

Lamplight Toad

The European green toad lives in the east of Europe and in the area from North Africa across to central Asia. In towns, these toads can be seen beneath street lamps waiting to catch insects attracted to the light.

There are more than 2,600 known species of frogs in the world today. The ancestors of modern frogs were the first backboned animals ever to live on land.

Super Jumper

A frog's powerful back legs are attached to a large pelvis, allowing the frog to jump almost 3 ft. Its short, stout front legs are firmly attached to its strong shoulders and absorb the shock when the frog lands.

The Fish

Fish are vertebrates. This means that they have a backbone and an internal skeleton, rather than an external, or outer, shell. Most fish live in water, breathe through gills, have a scaly body, and swim and move around by using their fins. Fish are cold-blooded. There are 20,000 species of fish living in the ocean, and 5,000 in rivers, lakes, and ponds.

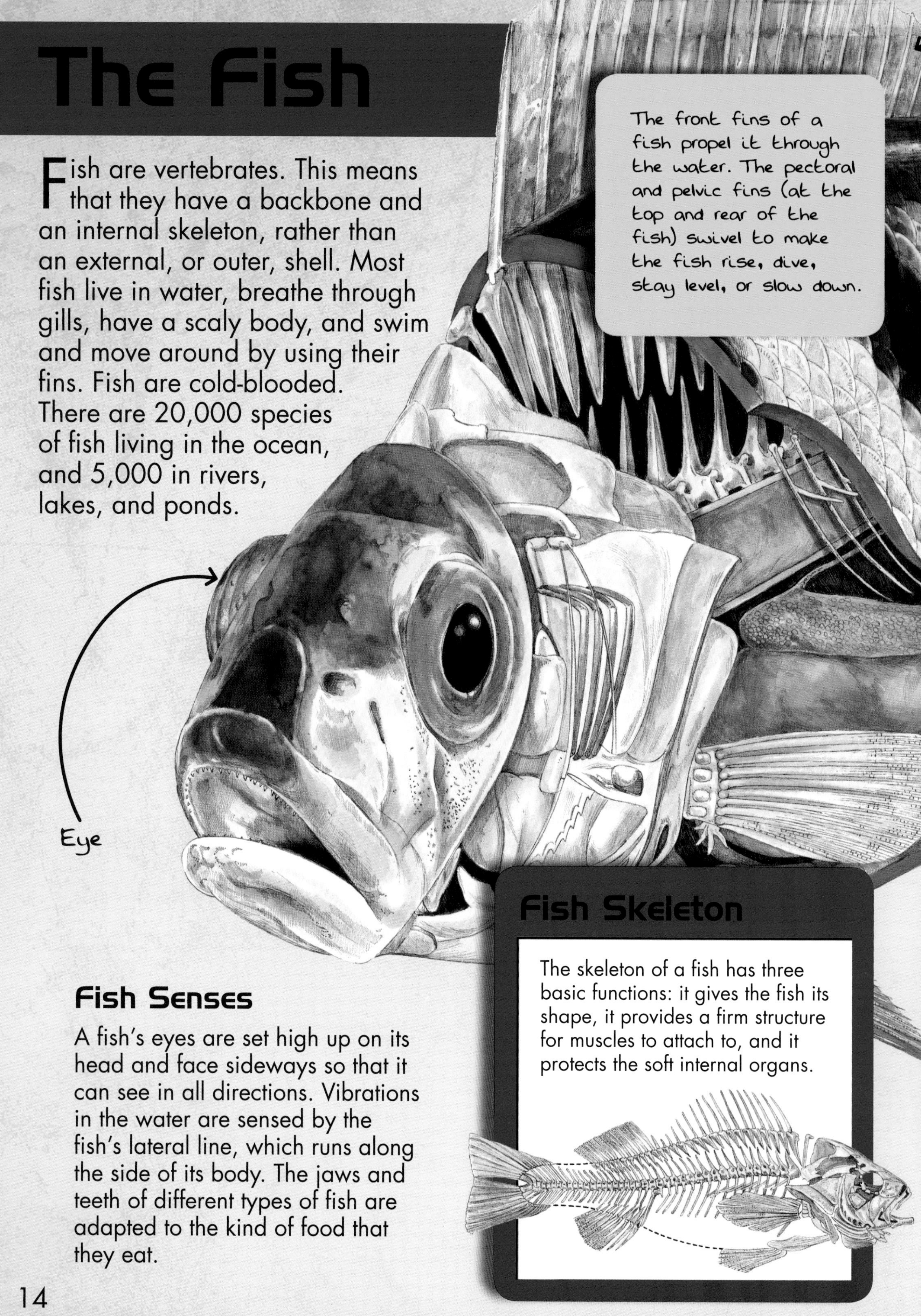

The front fins of a fish propel it through the water. The pectoral and pelvic fins (at the top and rear of the fish) swivel to make the fish rise, dive, stay level, or slow down.
Eye

Fish Senses

A fish's eyes are set high up on its head and face sideways so that it can see in all directions. Vibrations in the water are sensed by the fish's lateral line, which runs along the side of its body. The jaws and teeth of different types of fish are adapted to the kind of food that they eat.

Fish Skeleton

The skeleton of a fish has three basic functions: it gives the fish its shape, it provides a firm structure for muscles to attach to, and it protects the soft internal organs.

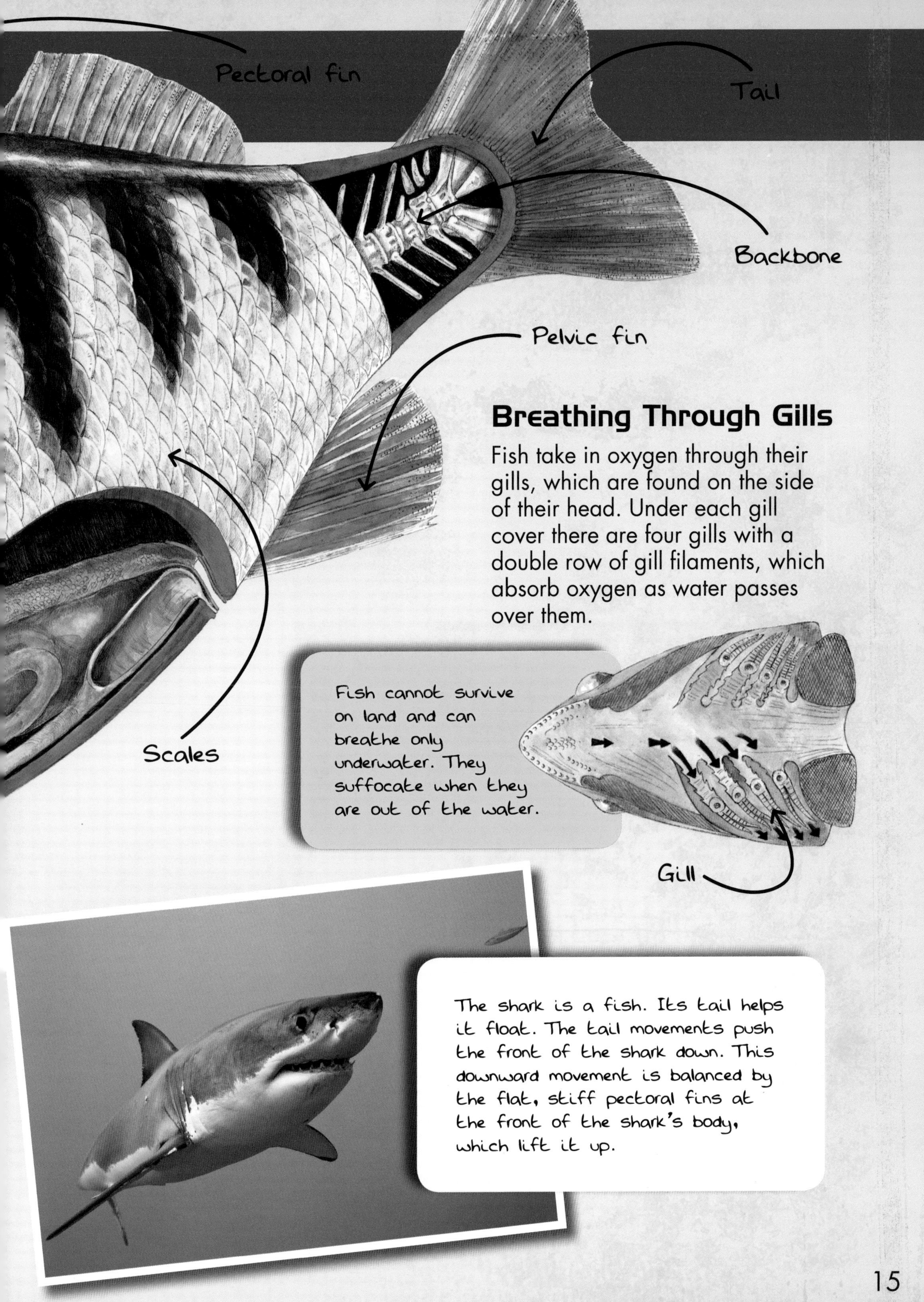

Breathing Through Gills

Fish take in oxygen through their gills, which are found on the side of their head. Under each gill cover there are four gills with a double row of gill filaments, which absorb oxygen as water passes over them.

Fish cannot survive on land and can breathe only underwater. They suffocate when they are out of the water.

The shark is a fish. Its tail helps it float. The tail movements push the front of the shark down. This downward movement is balanced by the flat, stiff pectoral fins at the front of the shark's body, which lift it up.

The Snake

The snake is a strange, legless reptile with a long, slender body. Scientists believe that snakes evolved from a type of burrowing lizard and have lost the need for legs along the way. A snake slithers on its belly. Its soft organs are contained inside a rib cage that stretches to its tail.

Giant Python

A large reticulated python can grow up to 33 ft (10 m) long and can swallow a deer or small pig. Boas and pythons live in trees. They suffocate their prey by wrapping their body around it before crushing it to death.

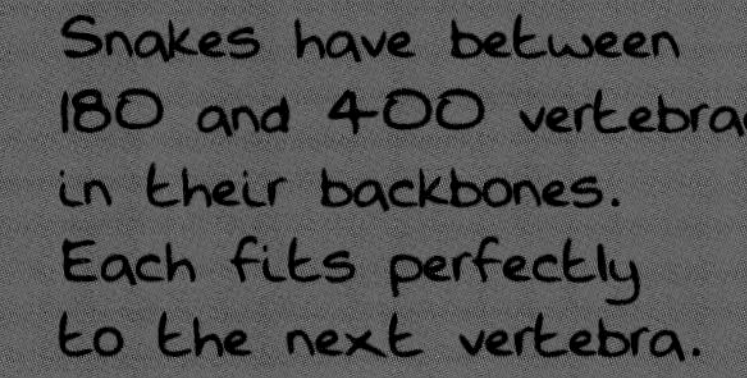

Snakes have between 180 and 400 vertebrae in their backbones. Each fits perfectly to the next vertebra.

Open Wide!

Some snakes have fangs. As the snake bites, its fangs inject deadly venom into prey. The venom paralyzes the prey so that it cannot move and then the snake eats it.

Fang

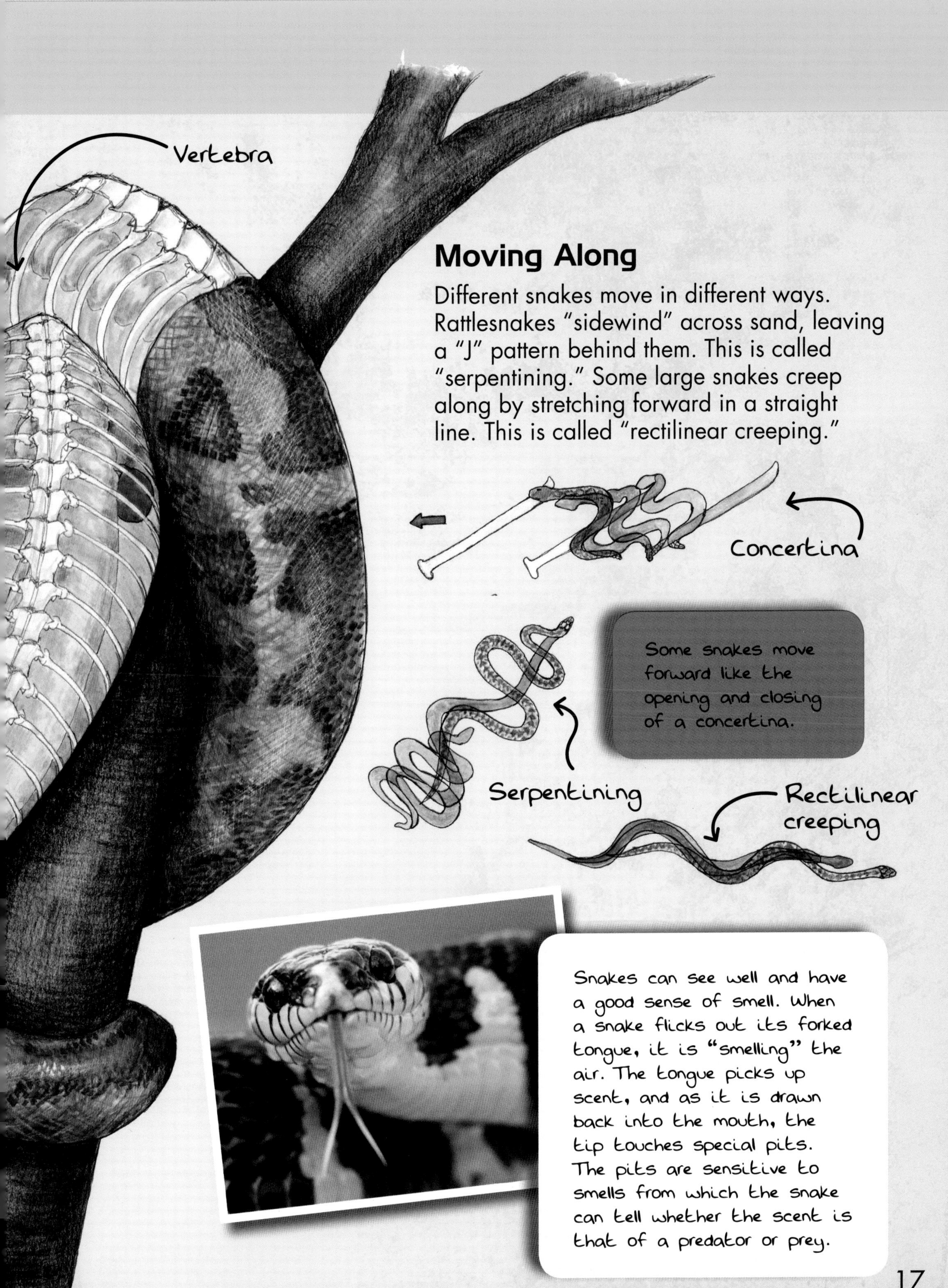

Moving Along

Different snakes move in different ways. Rattlesnakes "sidewind" across sand, leaving a "J" pattern behind them. This is called "serpentining." Some large snakes creep along by stretching forward in a straight line. This is called "rectilinear creeping."

Snakes can see well and have a good sense of smell. When a snake flicks out its forked tongue, it is "smelling" the air. The tongue picks up scent, and as it is drawn back into the mouth, the tip touches special pits. The pits are sensitive to smells from which the snake can tell whether the scent is that of a predator or prey.

The Bird

The bird is a member of a group of warm-blooded animals. Birds have two legs, a head with a beak, and two wings. Most birds, but not all, can fly, and all have feathers—no other creature in the animal kingdom has feathers. Feathers are important to the bird not just for flying, but also to keep the creature warm in extremely cold temperatures.

The feathers of many birds are brightly colored. Males often have striking colors and patterns, while females are very plain. Male birds display their feathers when they are trying to attract a mate.

Lightweight Flier

A bird's body, with its strong but lightweight skeleton, is an efficient flying machine. Its feathers are perfectly designed for flight. The thin barbs of the feather interlock to form a smooth airfoil surface that provides the lift needed for flight.

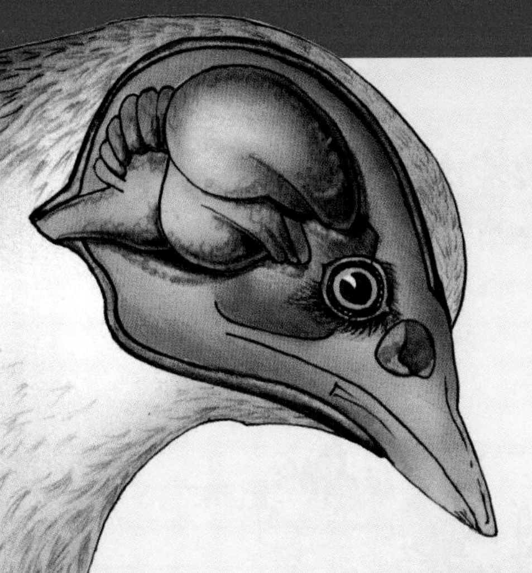

Hollow Bones

The long bones of a bird are hollow with delicate struts inside for extra strength. This lightweight structure allows the bird to fly easily and cope with rough landings.

The skeleton of a bird has evolved to suit its lifestyle. The backbone and limb girdles are designed to carry the weight of the bird's body as it walks or flies.

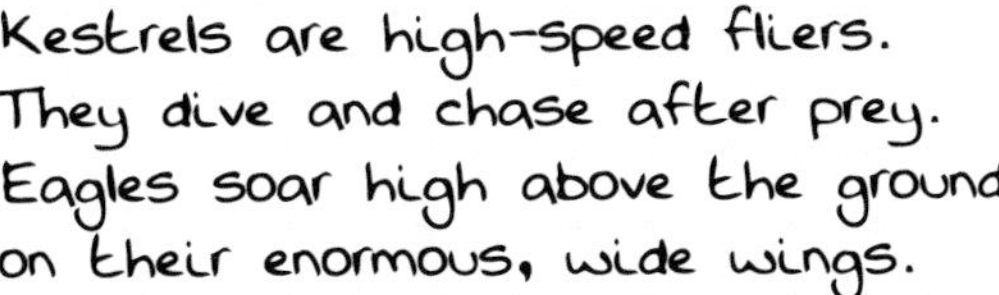

Kestrels are high-speed fliers. They dive and chase after prey. Eagles soar high above the ground on their enormous, wide wings.

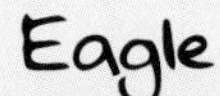

Eagle

Baby Birds

Birds lay eggs within which baby birds develop. It takes around 20 days for a baby bird to develop fully before it hatches from its egg. Just a few minutes after hatching, the baby can move around and eat.

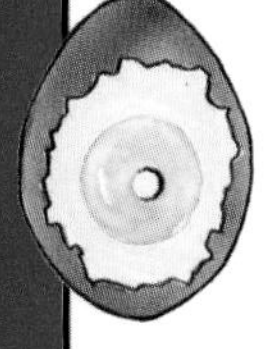
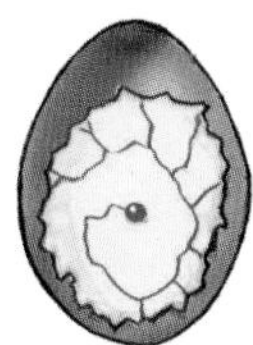
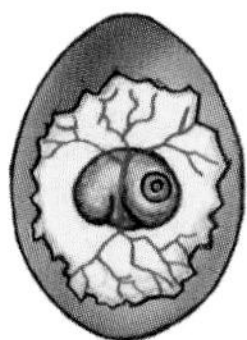
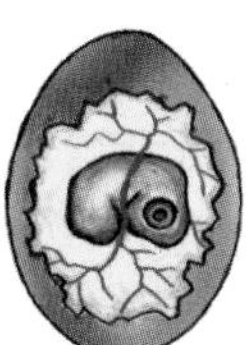

The Rat

Rats belong to a group of vertebrate animals called mammals. Most mammals have fur, are warm-blooded, and feed their young with milk from their body. There are around 4,000 species of mammals, including rats. Rats are very intelligent animals. They quickly learn where to find food and shelter and have adapted well to living near humans.

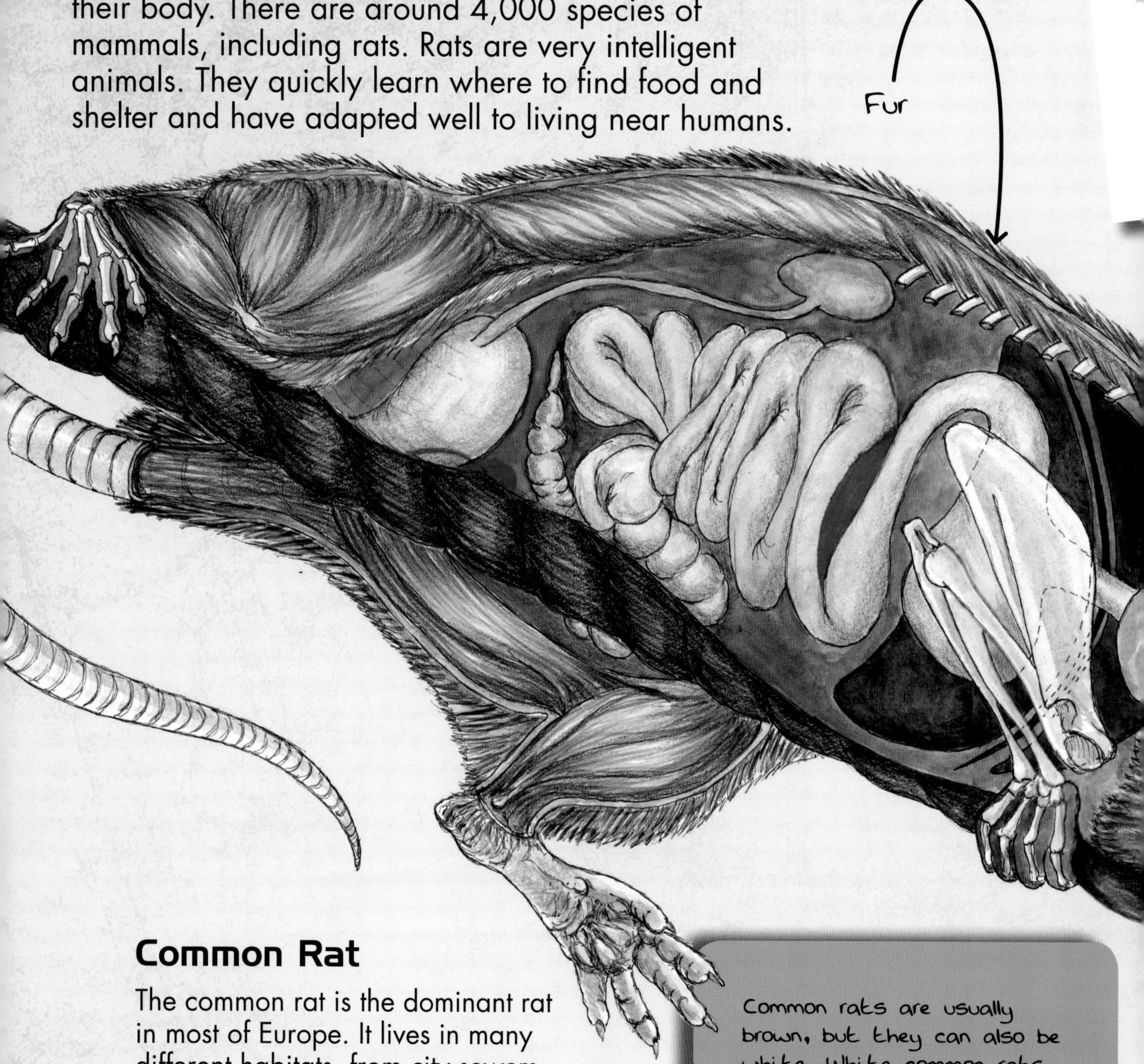

Common Rat

The common rat is the dominant rat in most of Europe. It lives in many different habitats, from city sewers and warehouses to farmyards. The rat can also live on rocky shores and in salt marshes.

Common rats are usually brown, but they can also be white. White common rats are the rats most often used in laboratory testing.

Black Rat

The black rat is found in warmer parts of the world. It has been introduced to cooler areas on ships. It is black or brown and has longer ears and a longer tail than the common rat.

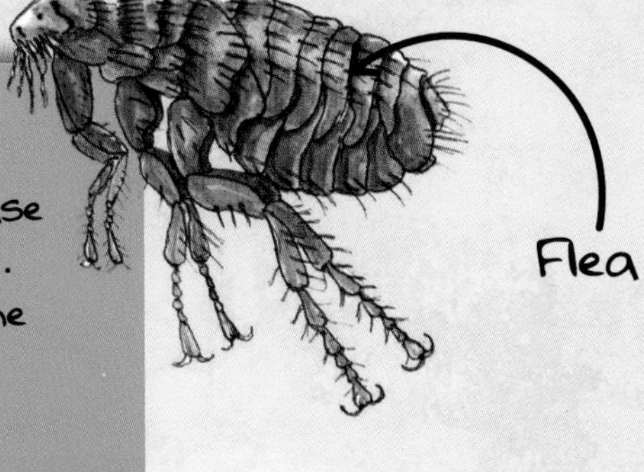

In the Middle Ages, rat fleas were responsible for spreading a terrible disease called the "Black Death," or the plague. Humans who came into contact with the rat's disease-carrying fleas were soon infected by it. The plague was highly contagious and killed many thousands of people around the world.

The rat's long, curved incisor teeth keep growing throughout its life. The teeth sharpen to chiseled points as they rub together.

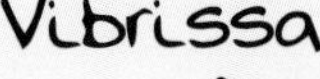

Rat Senses

Smell and touch play an important part in a rat's life. Its whiskers are called vibrissae and are sensitive to touch. The rat uses them to feel its way in the dark.

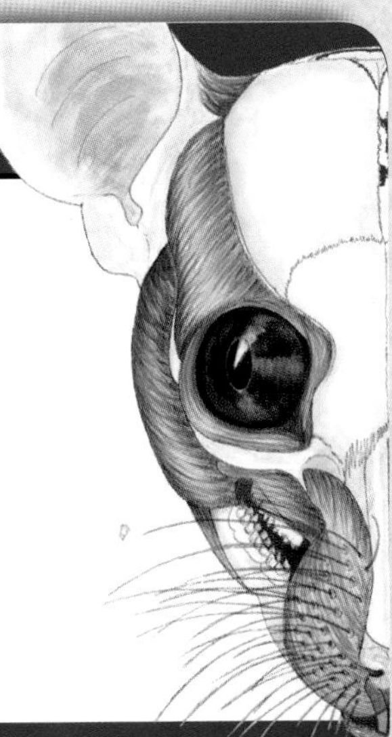

The Tiger

The tiger is a mammal. It is also a carnivore. It is part of a group of big cats that includes lions, cheetahs, jaguars, leopards, and panthers. Tigers live in parts of Asia, including India, Sumatra, Java, and Bali. Tigers have been hunted so much that some species are now extinct. The tiger is one of Earth's most endangered animals and is a protected species.

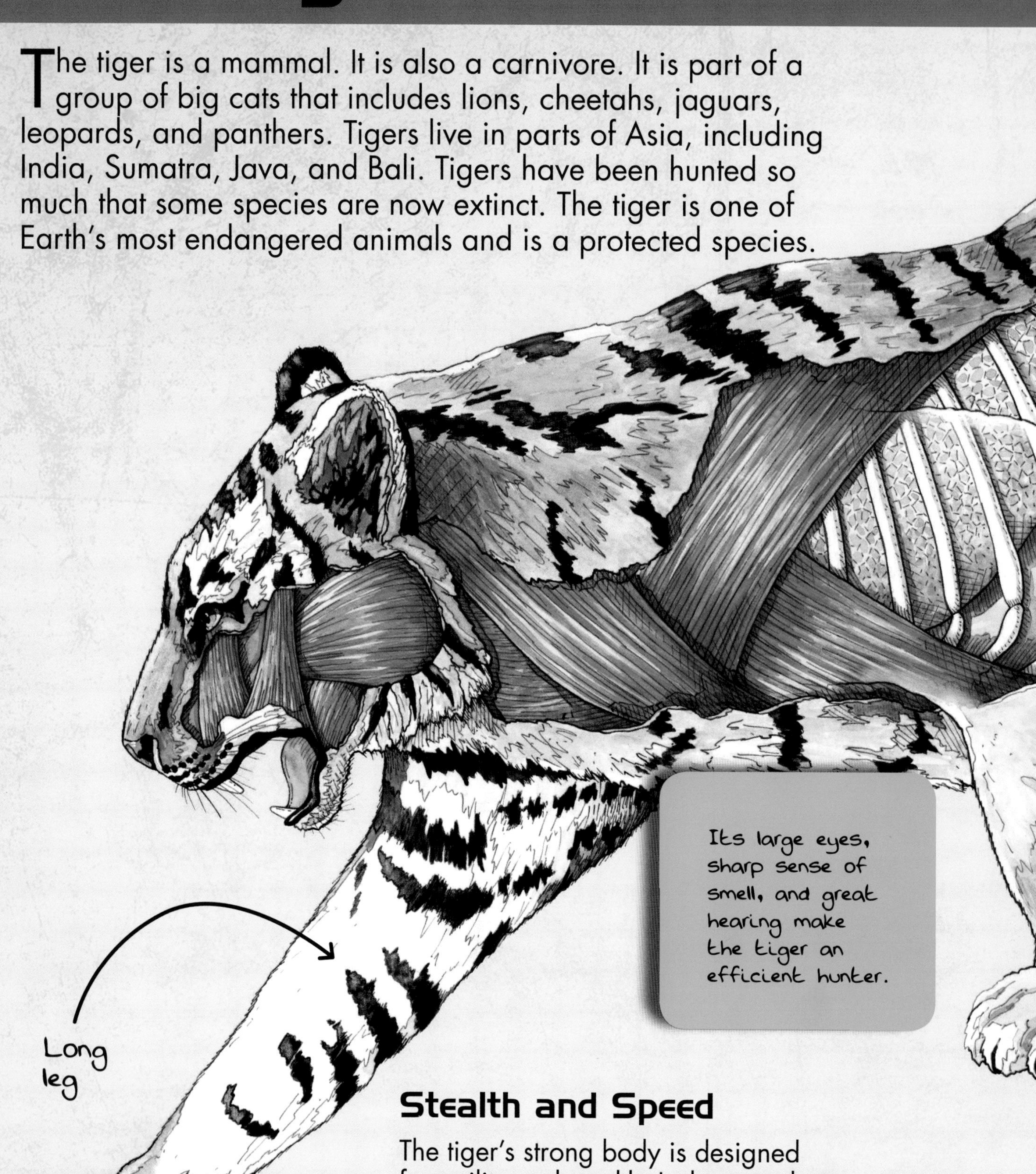

Its large eyes, sharp sense of smell, and great hearing make the tiger an efficient hunter.
Long leg

Stealth and Speed

The tiger's strong body is designed for agility and stealth. Its legs are long and its spine is very flexible. A long muscular tail helps the tiger balance as it runs or climbs. Unlike other big cats, the tiger is also a good swimmer and enjoys being in water.

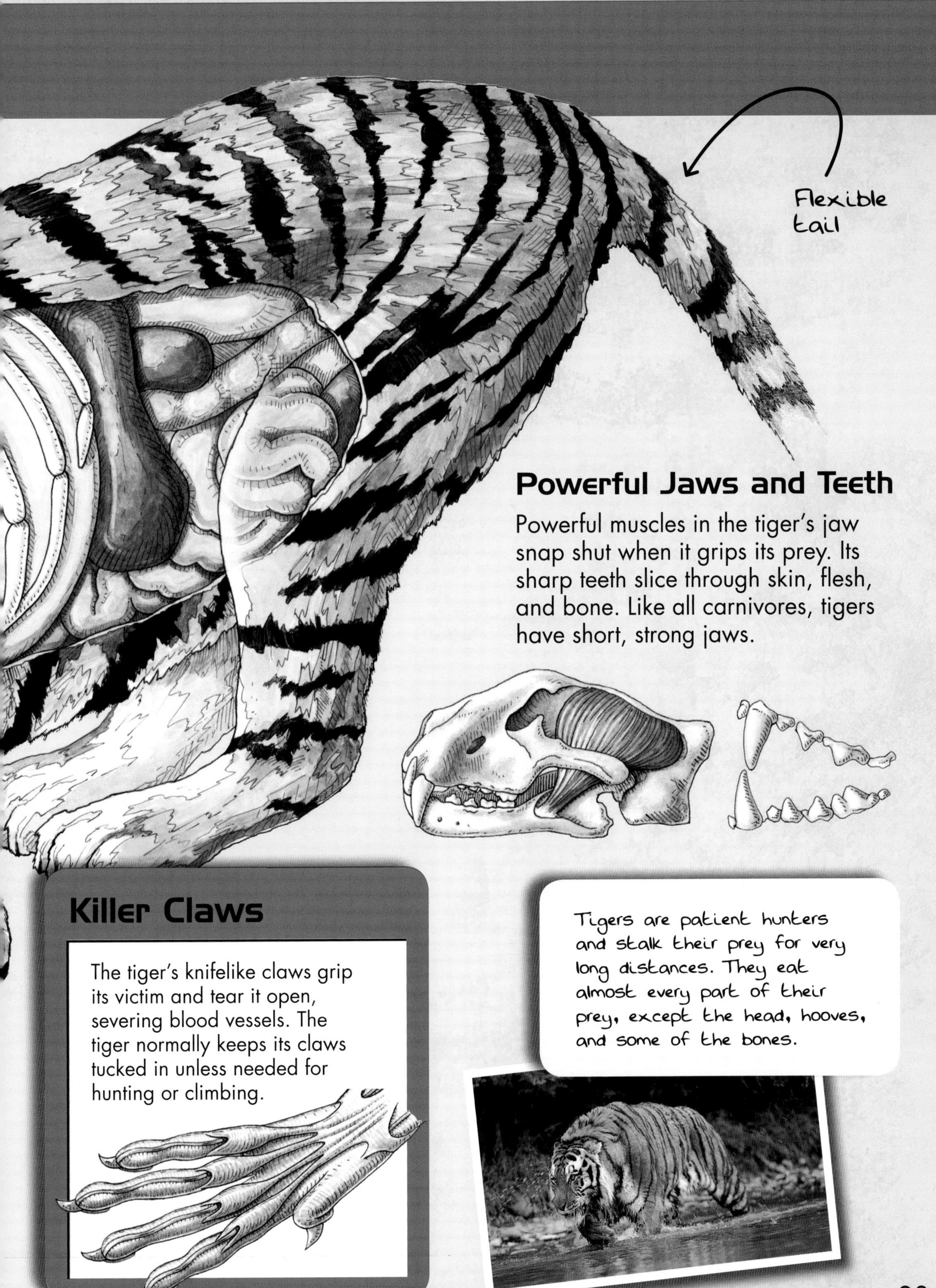

Powerful Jaws and Teeth

Powerful muscles in the tiger's jaw snap shut when it grips its prey. Its sharp teeth slice through skin, flesh, and bone. Like all carnivores, tigers have short, strong jaws.

Killer Claws

The tiger's knifelike claws grip its victim and tear it open, severing blood vessels. The tiger normally keeps its claws tucked in unless needed for hunting or climbing.

Tigers are patient hunters and stalk their prey for very long distances. They eat almost every part of their prey, except the head, hooves, and some of the bones.

The Elephant

The elephant is the largest land-living mammal on Earth today. It measures almost 13 ft (4 m) high and weighs around 13 tons (12 metric tons). Its massive body, huge head, large ears, long trunk, and curved tusks cannot be mistaken for those of any other animal. Elephants live in Africa and Asia. They are found in dense forests, savannas, desert scrublands, and river valleys.

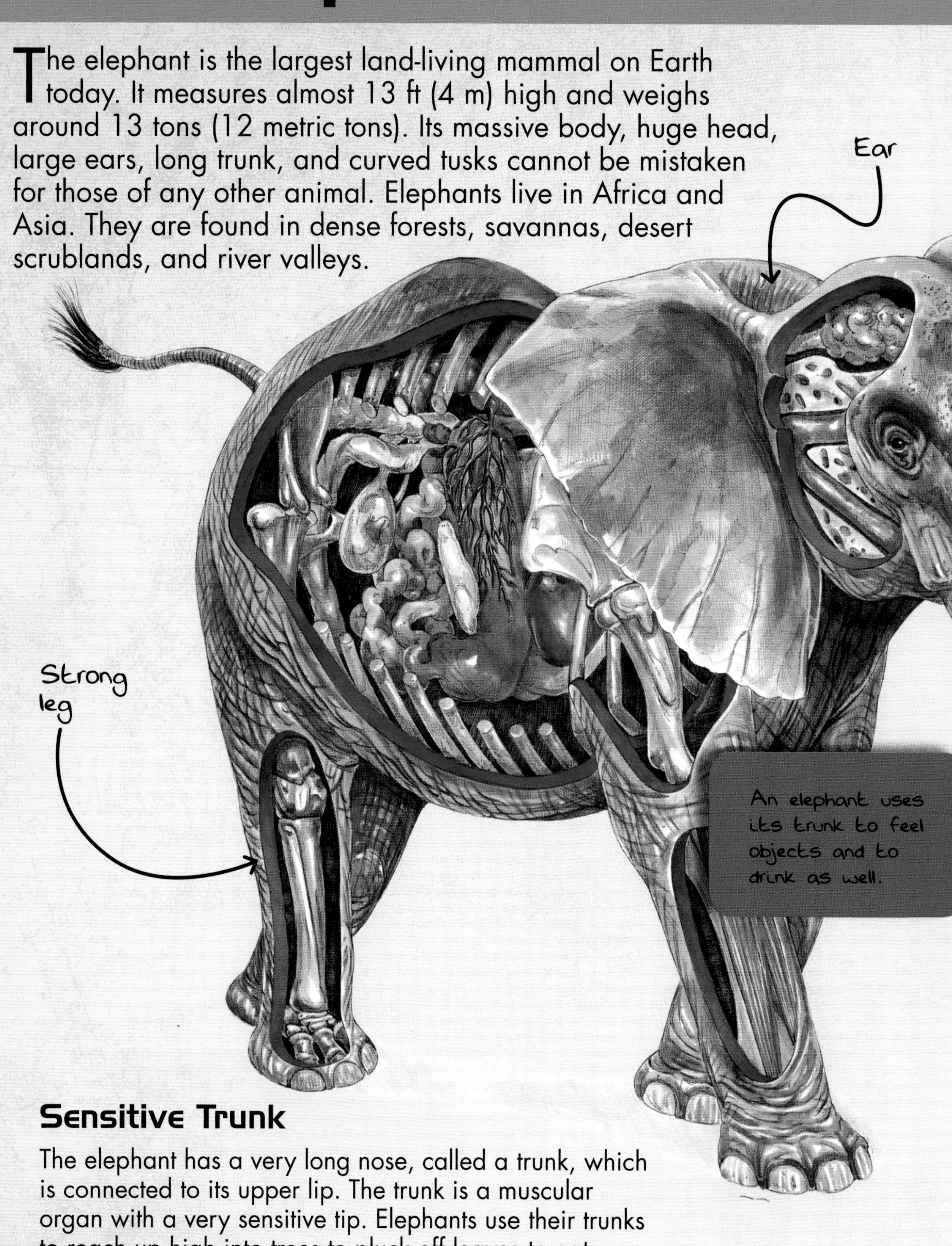

Ear
Strong leg
An elephant uses its trunk to feel objects and to drink as well.

Sensitive Trunk

The elephant has a very long nose, called a trunk, which is connected to its upper lip. The trunk is a muscular organ with a very sensitive tip. Elephants use their trunks to reach up high into trees to pluck off leaves to eat.

Elephants will charge at anything that threatens or annoys them. A charging elephant can be deadly.

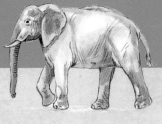

Heavyweight Runner

The elephant's backbone acts as a rigid girder, which balances the weight of its body with the weight of its head. An elephant's weight is supported on four enormous legs. Elephants move slowly most of the time, but when necessary, these animals can run at a surprisingly fast speed.

An elephant cleans itself by using a "dry shampoo" technique. It sucks up dust through its trunk, then blows it all over its body. The elephant then rubs the dust in, scratches, and shakes—this removes any dirt and bugs from the skin.

Trunk

Radiator Ears

The elephant's huge ears act like radiators. They have fine blood vessels located just below the surface of the skin. When the elephant flaps its ears, these blood vessels lose heat easily and prevent the elephant from overheating.

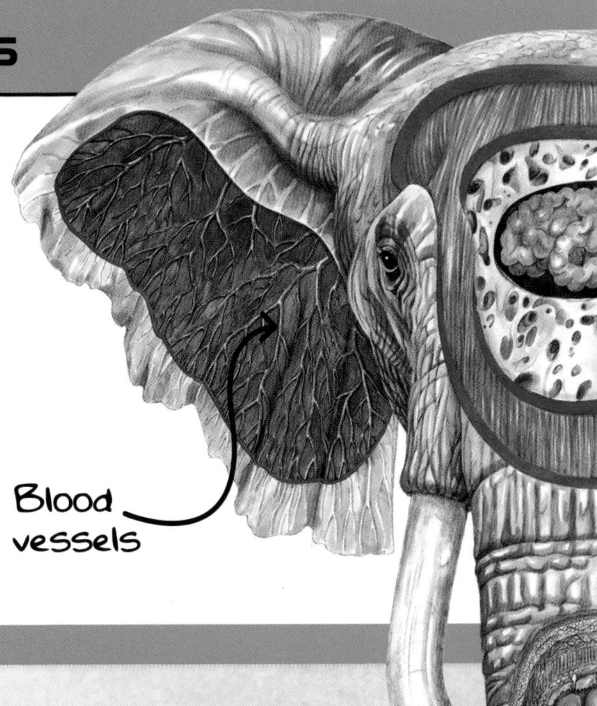

The Whale

Whales are mammals that spend their entire lives in the ocean. Like dolphins and porpoises, whales are cetaceans. The earliest cetaceans appeared on Earth 50 million years ago. The ancestors of whales were land-based animals with legs and feet. They evolved over time to become sea-living animals with a pair of flippers instead of legs.

Many whales have callosities, or horny growths, on their head in which worms and whale lice live.

Staying Warm

Like all mammals, whales are warm-blooded. The whale has a layer of fatty tissue, called blubber, beneath its skin. Blubber keeps it warm in cold waters. In some whales, the layer of blubber can be up to 20 in (50 cm) thick.

As the whale evolved from a land-living animal to a sea-living animal, its nostrils moved from the front of its head to the top of its head. It became just one hole—the blowhole.

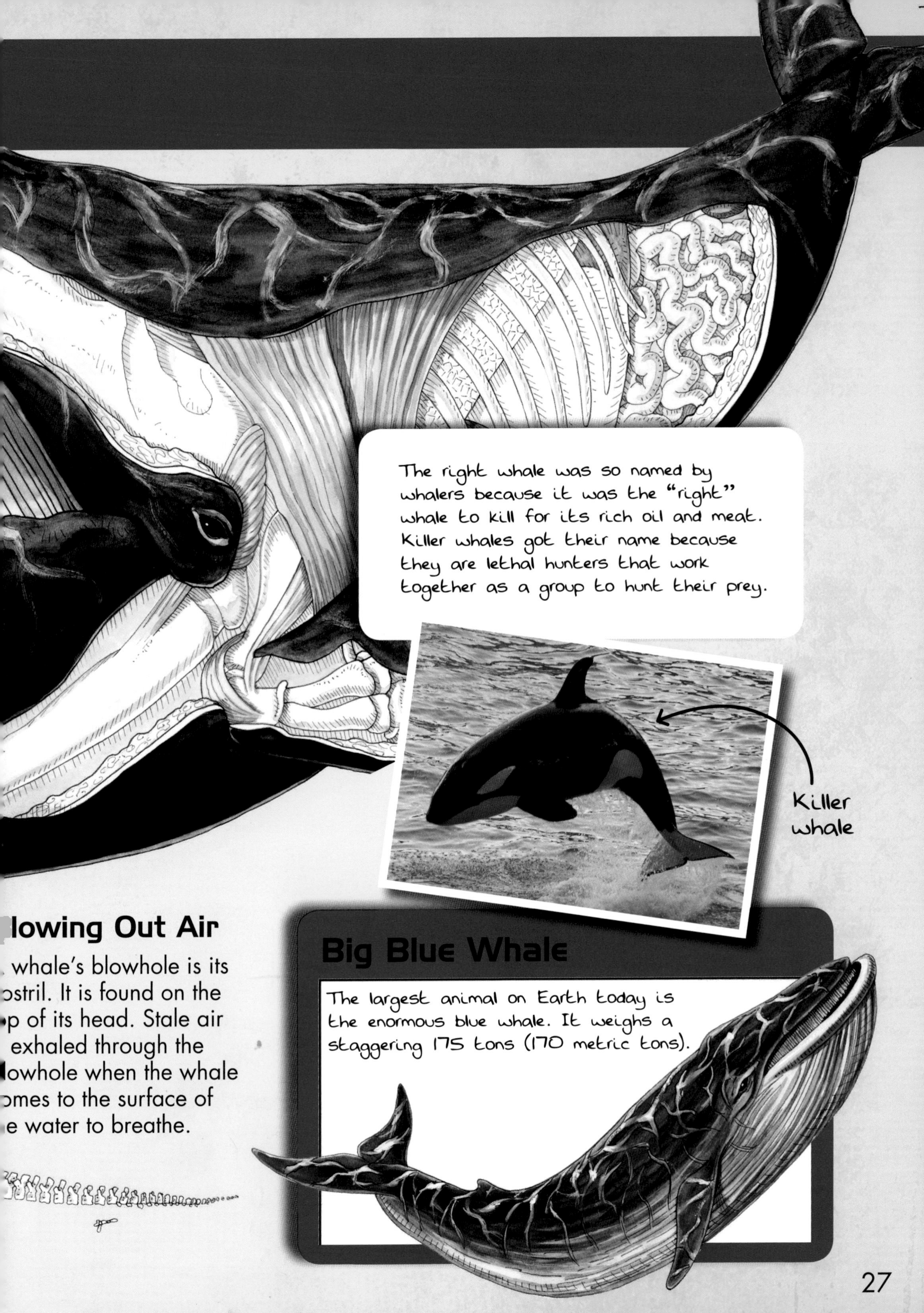

The right whale was so named by whalers because it was the "right" whale to kill for its rich oil and meat. Killer whales got their name because they are lethal hunters that work together as a group to hunt their prey.
Killer whale

lowing Out Air

whale's blowhole is its ostril. It is found on the p of its head. Stale air exhaled through the lowhole when the whale omes to the surface of e water to breathe.

Big Blue Whale

The largest animal on Earth today is the enormous blue whale. It weighs a staggering 175 tons (170 metric tons).

Amazing Animal Facts

Caterpillar Change

Butterflies are insects that begin their lives as caterpillars. The process they go through to change from a caterpillar into a butterfly is called metamorphosis.

Strange Salamander

The axolotl is an amphibian. It is a salamander that looks like an overgrown tadpole! It even has feathery gills like a tadpole. It remains in its larval form throughout its life and even breeds in this form.

Killer Sharks

The shark is a fish. Sharks will attack penguins, birds, seals, dolphins, crabs, squid, and even other sharks. Their teeth are constantly replaced, and there may be more than one row of teeth in the mouth at one time.

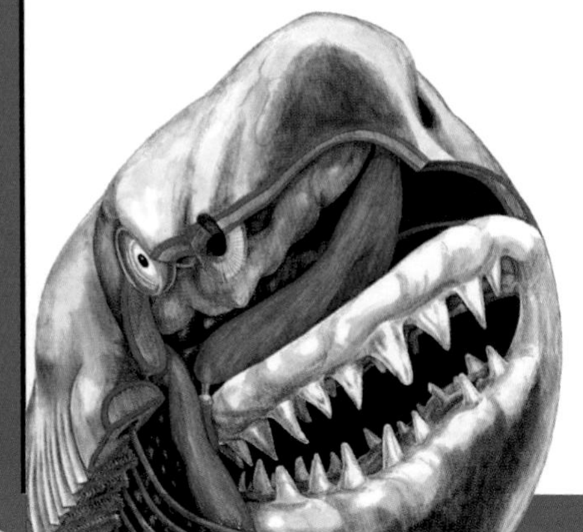

Ink Squirter

Octopuses and squid are mollusks. They squirt ink from their anus when they are frightened. The ink helps hide the creature from predators, allowing it to swim away unseen.

Great Flier

The arctic tern is a bird and a superb long-distance flier. During its lifetime, the bird may travel more than 155,000 miles (250,000 km)!

Komodo Killer

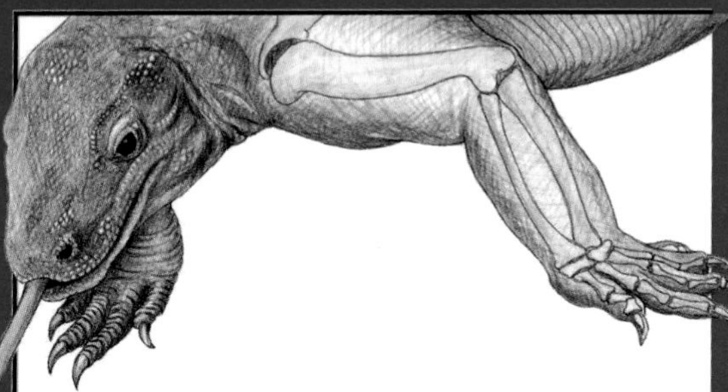

The Komodo dragon is a reptile and the world's largest lizard. It can grow up to 10 ft (3.1 m) long. It kills its prey by delivering a poisonous bite. The prey then becomes paralyzed and eventually dies. The Komodo dragon then eats it.

Flying Squirrel

The flying squirrel is a mammal. The skin between its front arms and hind legs stretches out to form a winglike shape that allows the squirrel to "fly" from tree to tree. The squirrel's tail acts as a rudder to help it steer and as a brake to help it stop!

Super Sprinter

Cheetahs are mammals. They can reach speeds of more than 68 mph (110 kph) when chasing after prey. The cheetah is the fastest land animal on Earth.

Glossary

Airfoil an object shaped to produce an upward movement (lift) when it passes through a flow of water or air.

Carnivore an animal that eats meat.

Defecates poops, or gets rid of waste.

Evolved changed over a long period of time.

Incisor the sharp, chisel-like front tooth of a mammal.

Larval the first stage of an insect's life cycle when it is different from an adult but able to fend for itself.

Plague a deadly epidemic or disease that sweeps quickly through an entire population.

Predator an animal that catches other animals for food.

Prey an animal that is, or may be, eaten by another.

Savanna an area of flat, level land that is covered with low plants such as grass, and that is usually treeless or dotted with trees and small woods.

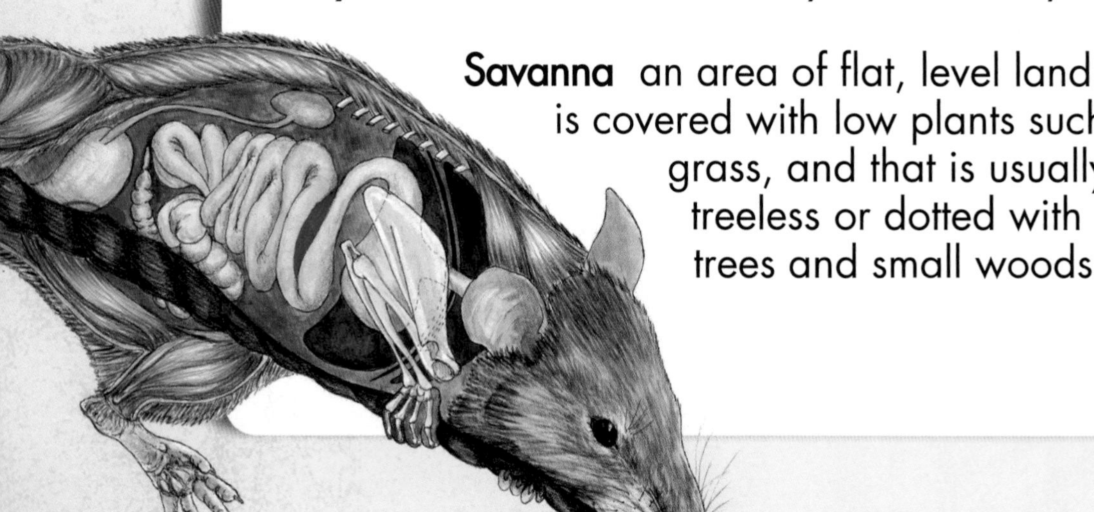

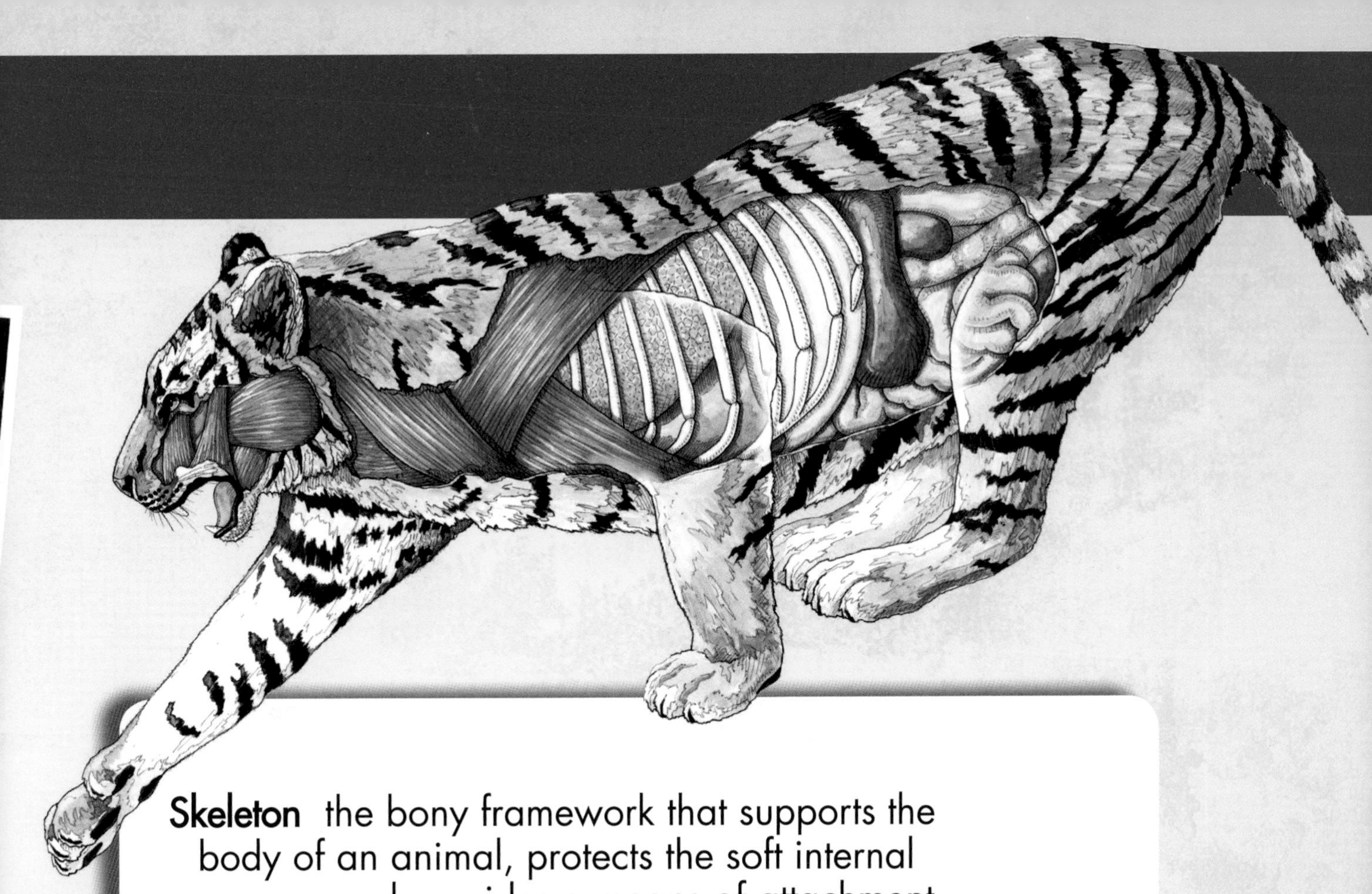

Skeleton the bony framework that supports the body of an animal, protects the soft internal organs, and provides a means of attachment for muscles and other tissues.

Species a group of similar animals that can breed with one another but that are incapable of breeding with other species.

Venom the poison produced by some animals and plants as a means of defense or attack.

Vertebrate an animal that has a bony internal support also known as a backbone.

Webbed a term used to describe the feet of some animals the toes of which are connected by a membrane.

Index